Stuff and Nonsense

A Book of Verse for Children

by John Dean

with illustrations

by Erik Sansom

John Dean

HB
HARVEY BOOKS

Stuff and Nonsense © 2006 John Dean.
johnmichaeldean@yahoo.co.uk

Published by Harvey Books.
First Edition 2006.

Illustrations by Erik Sansom.
esansom@sympatico.ca

Typeset by Publishing Solutions.
Printed in Sweden by Kristianstad Book Printers.
One of the world's most environmentally friendly companies.
www.kristianstad.co.uk

ISBN 0-946988-80-3
978 0 946988 80 8

For Lucy and Tom

Acknowledgements

To Lynne Dadley, whose actions prompted me to compile this collection.

To my daughter, Lucy, for her assistance in editing.

To William Roe, for his assistance in editing and for his suggestion
that I should include *About the Author* on the back cover.

To Victoria Smith, for her assistance in editing and for
providing me with the title *Little Dippy Dora*.

To Tony Coales, for assisting with grammar and punctuation.

To Jacqueline Lowery, for providing the
inspiration behind *I hate the letter "n."*

To Jonathan Boughtwood, for technical assistance.

To Kevin Inskip, for providing me with the title *Giggling Gertie*.

To the staff at Cosham Library, for their assistance.

Contents

for young ones

for older ones

Introduction

I have been writing rhyming versions of jokes, amusing quips and light-hearted poems for over thirty years. Some of the entries in this collection date back to the seventies and eighties, but many have been written over the past few months.

Since these verses have been designed for children there is a small educational element to be found along with an occasional hint of something serious, but this is mainly to be seen as a book of fun. I decided to divide the work into three sections suitable to different age groups, but I have not been specific about these age groups and there is nothing in the book that is unsuitable for any age. It is intended to be a collection that a person might delve into throughout their childhood and it may even encourage older children to read and entertain younger ones.

I have published this book myself and am hoping that with recognition I will achieve further publication. So if you enjoy the collection it would assist my cause if you could send an e-mail with your comments.

Have fun,

John Dean.
johnmichaeldean@yahoo.co.uk

for younger ones

Meddling with molluscs

My brother and I like racing snails –
They're slow, but show persistence.
And when my brother isn't looking
I can offer mine assistance.

It passes time in the garden
And it's harmless, I suppose –
And when I'm bored I pick one up
And stick it on my nose.

I want to fly off to Disney

I want to fly off to Disney,
But Mum says we can't go there yet.
What I'd give to be on that runway,
To be zooming away on that jet.

Mum says that taking a baby abroad
Is worrying, hard and unkind.
Well, I've got the perfect solution –
Why don't we leave her behind?

Diddley Squat

I used to have an invisible friend,
I called him Diddley Squat.
When I was feeling lonely
He helped me out a lot.

I played with him at weekends,
He would never let me down,
He would always come out smiling,
He would never let me frown.

But now I've got a real mate
To fill the vacant spot –
Hello, proper friendship!
Goodbye, Diddley Squat!

Swaps

I had a peacock feather,
A dry squashed worm called Scott,
A key I found
Beneath the ground –
One marble bought the lot.

A Little boy like me

I saw him on the news last night,
A little boy like me –
Six or seven, maybe eight,
Underfed and underweight,
But a little boy like me.

He had nothing, not a thing,
That little boy like me –
Begging there upon his knees,
And I have all there is to please
A little boy like me.

I thought of him again today,
The little boy like me –
No family, no place to live,
No one to play and tussle with -
That little boy like me.

A world away from luxury,
A little boy like me –
Poor and sad and thin and ill,
No one to love him there, but still
A little boy like me.

Attack! Attack!

My sister has these head lice;
They're crab-like little things;
They run around upon her scalp –
I'm glad they don't have wings!

Diddle Dankin

By the pond beneath a tree
Lived a gnome of gentle style.
To his grave then let us walk
And think of him awhile.

His name was Diddle Dankin,
But his famous gnome de plume
Was Laugh-Alotty-Not-I-Worry-
Never-Want-Nor-Fume.

His statue is his gravestone
And his cheeky little grin
Indicates a wealth of good
And a minimum of sin.

In life he offered pleasure,
A feast of fun and joy –
And this he gave, despite his faults,
To every girl and boy.

On rainy days and sunny days,
No matter what the clock,
Around old Diddle Dankin
The children would a-flock.

They watched him jump and skip,
Watched him reel and roll,
They laughed and clapped and cried,
"Oh, the clever little soul!"

Some have said he should have found
More useful things to do.
I say: "To spread some happiness
Is to live your life!" – Don't you?

My cousin sucks her thumb

My cousin sucks her thumb,
She makes it fat and gummy.
She's been doing it ever since
She stopped sucking at her mummy.

I am black and you are white

I am black and you are white,
All my bits are screwed on tight,
Yours too are firmly held in place –
What is this thing that they call "race?"

Please don't give me sprouts

Please don't give me sprouts,
They taste like soggy soap.
If you say I have to eat them
I'll just sit around and mope.

They really are disgusting
And they give us wind, I think –
The dog ate some last Christmas
And did he make a stink!

If I was on a desert island,
Just me and a giant sprout,
When it came to choosing what to eat
I would plump for nowt.

It's okay

It's okay to wear glasses,
It's okay being bald,
It's okay to have – oh, whatever
That weird condition's called!

It's okay being black,
It's okay being white,
It's okay to stay in all day
Or to stay out till late at night.

It's okay having crooked teeth,
It's okay having braces;
It's okay looking serious,
But it's okay making faces.

I'm okay with everything,
It's quite all right with me –
It is a free world, after all,
So I say, "Just feel free!"

Fluff up my pillow

Fluff up my pillow,
Tuck me in at night,
Stop me from worrying,
Try to make things right.

I don't want to be bullied,
Please keep me from the pain,
Make me feel so comfortable
That I won't get hurt again.

My pop up book of spots

It is quite realistic,
Great big spots jump from within.
There is a page that has a dozen spots
On a protruding chin.

And there is one revolting spot,
If you had it you would die,
And when you squeeze it hard enough
Pus shoots up in your eye.

A furry pig

A furry pig I would sit and stroke,
It would be so very cute.
A furry pig we would not harm,
We would not slice, not shoot.

But since the pig has no fur
We exploit it – such a sin!
And it's a good job human beings
Use clothes to cover skin.

The Dreadful Sisters Grimm

They stare at me at playtime –
The Dreadful Sisters Grimm.
And when my friend walks passed them
They turn their stare on him.

It seems that other people
Are inferior to them
For every action that they witness
They instantly condemn.

When I slip or trip or stumble,
When I seem a little dim,
I expect them to be watching –
The Dreadful Sisters Grimm.

Give your cat a gander

Give your cat a gander –
Come on, don't be a wuss!
And if it eats it all it will become
A duck-filled fatty puss!

Mark and Frankie

Through the streets at midnight
The dreadful duo glide.
One is Mark, the Minstrel's son –
The other, Frankie Hyde.

Those who know them keep away,
They never dare to stare
At the two most gruesome ghastly ghouls
In Pseudo San Benare.

Flying by the windows,
Feeling at the ground,
Mark and Frankie hanky-panky
Everywhere around.

Utter not a whisper,
Hide beneath a friend,
But the pesky pair will come along
And find you in the end.

Flying by the windows,
Feeling at the ground,
Mark and Frankie hanky-panky
Everywhere around.

Here they come, my darling,
Drifting through the air –
The two most gruesome ghastly ghouls
In Pseudo San Benare.

When Grandma grows a beard

She didn't have one last year,
Her skin was soft and smooth –
Now there are tiny tufts of hair
Sticking out of every groove.

It really is unusual
And at the very least it's weird –
And you begin to question everything
When Grandma grows a beard.

The wart on Nanny's nose

My grandparents are good to me –
They buy me food and clothes.
It's just that I am bothered by
The wart on Nanny's nose.

It is a colossal size
And every year it grows.
One day it will engulf the world –
The wart on Nanny's nose.

My life is full of promise,
I'm fit from head to toes,
But only if it wasn't for
The wart on Nanny's nose.

Awakening

One day I woke to find myself
Much smaller than a flea
And all the little toys of mine
Seemed mountainous to me.

From my giant plateau of a bed
I peered down to the floor
And muttered, "Ah, so this is what
The vacuum cleaner's for!" –

Enormous clumps of grit and fluff
In long unsightly rows,
And I knew then why my father said
I mustn't pick my nose.

I thought I'd go and gain
Some comfort from my bear,
But sitting vast before me
He didn't see me there.

A bed bug crawled towards me saying,
"Will you take me for a pet?"
"I'd rather not," was my reply,
"I hardly know you yet!"

Then my Mum boomed from the landing,
"Come on, get out of bed!"
I answered with a tiny squeak,
"Can you pick me up instead?"

I knew she couldn't hear me,
I'd have to climb down to the floor,
But then I saw a monster
Standing over by the door –

A spider many times my size,
With legs all long and thin –
He looked at me and offered up
A sly and evil grin.

I nearly had to holler,
I nearly had to scream –
It's a good job I woke up again
And found it was a dream.

Aunts Millicent and Daphne

Aunts Millicent and Daphne,
They seem to have such fun,
They open up their garden
And play with everyone.

They have a trampoline, a slide, a swing
And games with balls and bats –
And they only ask you, which is fair,
Not to aggravate their cats.

Aunt Millicent lifts her skirt
And runs around like mad.
Aunt Daphne does a cartwheel,
Which really isn't bad.

Neither of them married,
They're sisters and they're great –
They say they both want husbands,
But it's obviously too late.

With tea and cakes and laughter
And ice creams cone by cone –
It's just a shame that they never had
Some children of their own.

Funny things these feelings

Funny things these feelings,
I get them every day:
I feel like being silly,
I feel I want to play,
I feel like doing nothing,
I feel I want to cry,
Sometimes on a Sunday
I feel I want to die,
I feel the need to worry,
I feel frightened sometimes too –
But it helps to share these feelings
With someone nice like you.

I love my little brother

I love my little brother.
I'm five and he is two.
I love him because I can tell him
Exactly what to do.

The Queen and King
of Backward Land

The Queen and King of Backward Land
Are nearing the front door,
But they are further now away from me
Than they were a step before.

The Queen is really not that old,
Some fifty years or so,
Which is younger by twelve whole months
Than she was a year ago.

And the King, with his stately beard
Flowing down his back –
Why, he's so old that the hairs of it
Are turning charcoal black.

Reigning in their land of fun,
This retrospective pair,
Their agreements to argue out,
Their differences to share.

I'd love to live as they do,
Never having to be late,
Sleeping when it's school time,
O wouldn't it be great! –

I'd stand upon my backward throne
With rings upon my toes
And make my armies cross the seas
In topsy-turvy rows.

Before Newton invented gravity

Before Newton invented gravity
In a world of weightless ease
Thoughtful birds with clumsy limbs
Perched on supersonic trees
And dogs in gossamer kennels grinned
At one-way-projectile fleas.

All property was portable,
The sky was full of sea,
You could kick a ball to Africa,
The world was light and free –
So why did Newton spoil it all
With his silly gravity?

I've got this awful jumper

I've got this awful jumper,
A present from Aunt Pam –
She said it was expensive,
But the label read "Oxfam."

My mum says I'm a monkey

My mum says I'm a monkey
To generate such mess –
I keep telling her she's wrong,
But she's right, I must confess.

My bedroom is disgusting,
Like the floor in a chicken coop –
I'm more than just a monkey,
I'm much more like a troupe.

A robin in my garden

A robin in my garden,
He appears there when I need him,
He bobs along in front of me,
He tweets for me to feed him.

A visitor to my abode,
But most welcome as a guest,
With a friendly little birdie heart
Beneath his scarlet breast.

I come from Puddletown

I come from Puddletown,
I love it when it's wet,
I splash around all day long
And never feel regret.

If places had the names
Of where we want to be,
Apart from Paradise, Nevada,
This would be the place for me.

My teacher is so old

My teacher is so old
He should be in a museum –
Then on Parents' Night Mum and Dad
Would have to pay to see him.

If he's put inside a cabinet
Behind a pane of glass
Then nobody will hear him
When he's shouting at the class.

Whether pigs have wings

It might be worth considering,
Perhaps I might be right,
And perhaps those twirly tails of theirs
Are propellers late at night.

They might fly above our houses
When we are fast asleep,
Hover by our windows
And take a porcine peep.

So they keep their wings well hidden –
But I wouldn't put it passed them,
And you cannot be sure if I am wrong
Until you've been and asked them.

Treedomville

Welcome to my little wood,
I play here now and then,
My favourite trees to climb on,
My cosy little den –

Away from the fuss and the bustle
Where heart and nature unite,
With the squirrels and the insects,
Where living is simple and right.

Who needs enemies?

My friends say I'm a baby
And they like to make me cry,
But then I have to ask myself –
What sort of friends have I?

When you've got the runs

Tickles and jokes
And cuddles and puns –
Nothing can cheer you
When you've got the runs.

for young ones

My velociraptor

I went there in a time machine
And brought him back to Slough.
I did it with amazing ease,
But please don't ask me how.

He is a clever raptor,
He helps me with my French,
And when I take him to the park
He sits upon a bench.

He has become my buddy pal,
I worship him completely,
And life is full of fun right now
Until he decides to eat me.

The weary man of Burton

I met a man of Burton
A-walking up the road.
He wore a tie, but had no shirt on,
And he heaved a heavy load.

"O weary man of Burton,"
My troubled frame did cry,
"Why is it you've no shirt on
And yet you wear a tie?"

"The reasoning is simple,"
Puffed this ageing man in haste,
"Upon my side's a dimple
Smothered in salmon paste.

"Had a shirt been on my back –
And here there is no doubt –
The salmon might have turned it black,
Which often leads to gout.

"And besides, a shirt would irritate,
The tie is far afield,
And so I will retain this state
Until my side has healed."

In a jestful way of protest
I cautiously implied
That the wearing of a string vest
Might prove kindly to his side.

"Absolute buffoonery!"
He spluttered through a frown.
"Do you make a fool of me
Or take me for a clown?

"Through a hole the spot would grow
And fester to a head –
Within a day I'd lose a toe
And within a week be dead!"

And with that he tucked his tie in,
Straightened up his load,
And then with one almighty grin
He continued up the road.

I decided one thing certain
As he stumbled on his way:
That if I should go to Burton
I'll not prolong my stay.

Born within a haystack

Born within a haystack
On the twenty-third of June
He was taken for a supersonic
Maladjusted prune.

In his early days of infancy
He would flash from tree to tree
And bathe, when others cared to watch,
In the Little Custard Sea.

He was always bright and merry
In his land all dark and grey,
And some had hopes that he would grow
To lead his folks one day.

He had an air about him,
Of that there was no doubt,
And if you asked him nicely
He would soar and wave and pout.

He may have lacked intelligence
And often seemed quite dense,
But in such a harsh environment
His absurdity made sense.

The people flocked to see him;
They revelled in the fun;
Their boring lives of misery
Were in his sight undone.

But alas, he met with glory
At the early age of three,
When he fancied something good to eat
And had himself for tea.

The end of yet

"Are we nearly there?"
"We're nowhere near there yet!"
"Is my dinner ready?"
"It isn't ready yet!"

Throughout my long-lived childhood
I live in deep regret
Forever always waiting
For the end of yet.

I have a little puppy

I have a little puppy,
He sleeps upon his back,
And he snores away unceasingly
Once he hits the sack.

But I love my little puppy
And he deserves a break.
He certainly makes up for it
Whenever he's awake.

My uncle wears thick glasses

My uncle wears thick glasses.
He looks at me bug-eyed.
As a toddler when I met him
I cried and cried and cried.

It's not that he is nasty,
But his eyes can pierce the brain,
Reveal all inner secrets
And make you go insane.

Where dragons went

We studied myths and legends,
But one thing I didn't know:
When time moved on from then to now
Where did the dragons go?

I haven't seen one in the zoo
Or in a nature book
And they're never in the countryside
However much I look.

My teacher couldn't tell me,
She said, "I don't know where!"
To be honest I would have to say
She didn't really care.

I asked my mum, I asked my dad,
I even quizzed the cat –
But when I asked my Aunty Kate
She said, "Good question, that!

"And I can give an answer,"
She continued, "sit you down
And I'll tell you all about the place
That's known as Dragon Town.

"All the dragons of the world
Moved in there long ago.
It's a lovely place of wonder –
They keep it quiet, though.

"No knights to interfere with them,
They play and skip and prance,
And all day long, claw in claw,
They dance their dragon dance.

"Breathing at each other –
It keeps them warm at night –
Ten thousand fires burning,
It really is a sight.

"They flame-grill food with elegance
And dragonistic pride –
And no need to buy your fuel when
It's located there inside.

"It's nothing like the life I live
Where there's so little left to do –
It's a special town of happiness
Where wishes all come true.

"Ah yes, there's magic to be found
Where dragons fly and roam!" –
But I had to leave her then –
It was time to go back home.

I wish I could have asked her more
And she's been missing since that day –
My dad says some white-coated men
Have taken her away.

My manx cat

My manx cat looks so miserable
Beneath its cloud of gloom,
Sitting there for hours
Like some harbinger of doom.

No human I can think of
Can pull so sad a face,
And I think I know the reason –
It has no tail to chase.

The Muddlelins

Living beside the Frozerted Plains
In the land of Shivery-Gee
They had little notion
Of locomotion,
But their thoughts were wild and free.

Muddlelin by nature and Muddlelin by name
They lived the boring life,
Each spending the day
In a tiresome way
By eating green peas with a knife.

Their land was cold and miserable
And as wet as wet could be.
So, to ease the stress,
And to agonise less,
They would paddle in the warm Maston Sea.

They were short and solemn and serious things
With two hands, eight fingers, no thumbs –
They longed for a sky
With the Sun burning high,
But they were none too hot on their sums.

They numbered twenty-three in all,
But could only count to eight –
And this inability to learn
Would cause concern
And ultimately determine their fate.

Now as I suggested originally
The Muddlelins were not partial to movement,
But on a day –
It was the tenth of May –
There were signs of great improvement.

A Muddlelin by the name of Meg
Had let her fame abound.
She was strong and eager,
Had the will of a beaver
And her body was fat and round.

She announced to all upon that day,
"There is a greater purpose to seek!
You've suffered too long!
Be firm! Be strong! –
Not feeble and humble and meek.

"Let me take you across the Frozerted Plains
Away from this land of regret.
O cannot you see
That Shivery-Gee
Is far too gloomy and wet?

"I'm sure that beyond those inclement wastes
There's a land of feasting and fun,
Where misery ends,
Where foes are friends
And where the Earth is kissed by the Sun.

"I'm being," she concluded, "both instructive
And positively truthful and right!
Pray sit not and grieve –
Make preparations to leave
On this our inaugural flight!"

Now Meg was most influential –
The pride of Shivery-Gee –
And very soon,
By the second of June,
Every Muddlelin agreed to her plea.

So with plenty of knifes in their rucksacks
And some jumbo-sized packets of peas
They journeyed inland
Away from the sand,
From the rain and the cold coastal breeze.

And with Meg leading on they all ventured
Into the Frozerted Plains.
Every Muddlelin nose
Soon withered and froze,
But ambition gave warmth to their pains.

She led them through the Agitalent Storms
And under the Banquet of Bones,
Through the Terrible Lands
Of the Slithering Sands,
But there were no quips, no moans.

Weary and weathered they travelled
With only their dream as a guide.
Time dragged by,
Then, in mid-July,
When hope had all but died –

They reached the edge of a valley
In which a river flowed swiftly through.
"Well, I'll be shamed,"
Meg exclaimed,
"My words were right and true!

"See, there is my land of promise,
Across yon river she lies –
O here at last,
Exotic and vast,
Is the Muddlelins' rightful prize!"

And indeed below in the distance
Stood a tropical land of delight –
With palm trees and clover –
Sheer beauty all over –
In Meg's own words: "What a sight!"

"May I ask," said a clear-headed Muddelin
With a thin and thoughtful face,
"How are we to reach the other side
Of this fearsome river, long and wide,
Which moves at such a pace?"

Meg lost her smile immediately
And with eyes stretched east to west
She groaned, "Oh blow!
Oh dear! Oh no! –
How do we pass this test?"

Someone knew the answer
Amid the weary ranks –
"Far there," she cried,
"I have espied
A bridge that joins the banks!"

So with jubilation in their hearts
And cries of "Ho!" and "He!"
The Muddlelins ran
Towards the span
That linked the caught and free.

They scampered down to the valley floor –
Two miles below its top –
But at the base
Meg turned her face
And called for them to stop.

She had noticed a notice nailed to a tree –
It read: "Just two times four!
Near bridge holds eight
So tempt not fate
If your party be nine or more!"

"Before we cross the bridge," Meg called,
"We must know our full amount.
Well, all of you
Know what to do –
So come along then, count!"

Each counted the mass thrice over,
But according to the Muddleline trait
The answer they got –
Which right it was not –
Equalled the maximum tonnage of eight.

"Now listen, you seven," Meg bellowed,
"We can all cross over as one!
We are here! We are free!
Come walk now with me
From the shadows and into the Sun!"

But as all twenty-two followed over
Cried one, "Run on! Don't look!"
With them nearing half-way
He'd felt the structure sway
And they hurried it slipped and shook.

Under the weight the timbers broke
And the tottering bridge crashed down.
Meg whimpered and screamed
And it certainly seemed
That every Muddlelin would drown.

Yet somehow they bobbled together
And caught hold of the timber afloat;
And with the aid of loose reeds
And some packets of peas
They successfully constructed a boat.

Then safely downstream they all drifted
Towards the warm Maston Sea,
But during the immersion
Meg had had a conversion
On the subject of where they should be.

They landed at the mouth of the river
Looking totally bushed and pale –
Yet following their fall
At least they all
Had lived to tell the tale.

"Rejoice in our salvation!"
Cried Meg, "then follow me
Without delay
To find a way
Back home to Shivery-Gee."

The Muddlelin response was instinctive
And along the shore they all sped,
Stopping to sleep and for meals
And to gawk at the seals,
Each knowing they could have been dead.

Passed cliffs and caves and inlets,
Over moorland and mudflat and fen,
Towards their goal
Every Muddlelin soul
Moving nearer and nearer, and then –

Back within sight of their homeland –
So welcome it was to behold.
Meg shouted with glee,
"O Shivery-Gee,
Your miserable shores we enfold!"

And thankfully back to the old life,
Vowing never to wander again,
With knives full of peas
And the sea at their knees,
To laugh at the wind and the rain.

So at last peace and joy was established
In all things Muddleline –
And although a bit late
I am pleased to relate
That they have managed to count up to nine.

Living beside the Frozerted Plains
In the land of Shivery-Gee –
"Though it is tempting to roam,"
Says Meg, "the home
Is where the heart will always be."

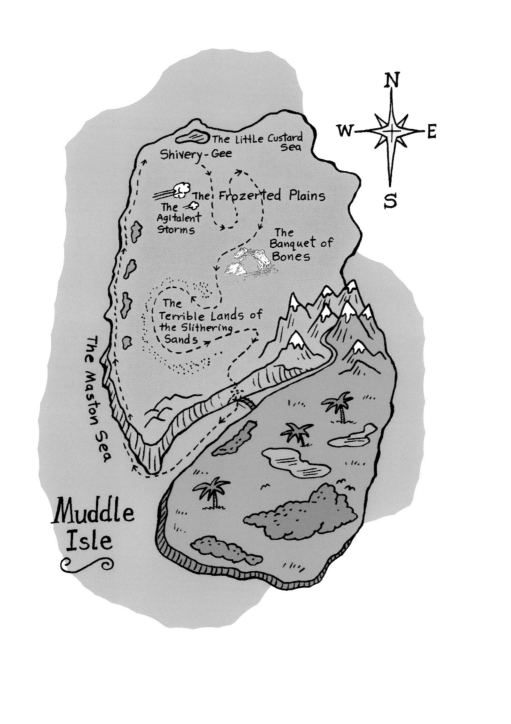

Billy No-Mates

Billy No-Mates plays alone,
In class no one sits near him.
Some say he is peculiar
And others even fear him.

He chats away to himself
Before and after lunch.
Some say he is the type of kid
That people ought to punch.

But when we were told in assembly
That a baby nearly died
And that Billy No-Mates saved her
I must admit I cried.

Billy No-Mates is a hero –
Why can't we all be friends?
From tomorrow morning
My mistreatment of him ends.

Unkempt, unloved, un-free

Beside a small and treasured well-gummed bone
A mermaid met a dog –
A whimsy dog,
A not so flimsy dog,
A grimsy and somewhat dimsy dog.

"A storm," she said, "has cast me out
From my world beneath the waves –
Those bumpy waves,
Those Neptunumpy waves,
Those over-humpy, non-aridumpy waves –

"And I need a being, strong, like you,
To take me to the shore –
To the glorious shore,
To the walrious shore,
To the to-jump-in-the-sea-is-what-it's-forious
        shore."

The dog, though somewhat overcome,
Kindly offered her his back –
His sturdy back,
His sheepherdie back,
His so-absurd-that-this-has-occuredy back.

And as he carried her she gently sang
Six verses of a song –
A wet skin of a song,
A non-din of a song,
An I'll-stroke-my-fin-on-your-chin of a song –

And her host was truly dogmatised
By the nature of her style –
Her swishy style,
Her splishy style,
Her half-dishy, semi-fishy style –

And as they neared the shore he pleaded,
"O marry me, sweet 'maid –
You scrumptious 'maid,
You sumptuous 'maid,
You lump not right to dumptuous 'maid!"

But unmoved she merely hopped away
And slithered down the beach –
That stony beach,
That lonely beach,
That life's-a-lot-of-baloney-beach.

The dog could only watch and whine
As she departed from the land –
That tall-trees-on land,
That dog-fleas-on land,
That ill-season, sad, no-reason land.

Now every month beside the sea
He bays beneath the Moon –
That fateful Moon,
That hateful Moon,
That far-too-late-a-date-for Moon –

Unkempt, unloved, un-free.

My little aide-mémoire

I always have it with me,
I keep it in a jar,
I find it very useful,
My little aide-mémoire.

It's very good with problems –
Unlike my Ma and Pa –
I cannot fault its reasoning,
My little aide-mémoire.

It helps me when I'm shopping,
When I'm late or in the car,
But I cannot tell you what it is,
My little aide-mémoire.

Without it I would lose my thread
And merely say "Blah! Blah!"
Oh yes, it really helps me through,
My little aide-mémoire.

Please don't give me bacon

Please don't give me bacon,
It sticks between my teeth –
So let me have something else
Unless you want to cause me grief.

After English breakfast
Strands of fat and rind
Dangling there disgustingly
Is what I always find.

And every time I smile
People see what I've been fed.
So please don't give me bacon –
I'll have orange juice instead.

Will I turn into my dad?

Will I turn into my dad? –
Combing over three hairs on my head,
Wearing slippers to nip to the shops,
Going up at nine-thirty to bed,
Falling asleep after dinner,
Dressing in sad, dreary clothes,
Growing hair right down my back
And out of my ears and my nose,
Complaining about everything modern –
So constantly grumpy and glum.

Perhaps I ought to consider
Turning into my mum.

The dashing man of Thornaby

A dashing man of Thornaby
Passed by my house one day.
On a lengthy lead he walked a flea
A shade of bluish-grey.

"O dashing man of Thornaby,"
I called in anxious awe,
"As if a pet you walk that flea –
What is the reason for?"

"I make no habit of it,"
He said through beaming smile,
"But it's because I own a closet
Of ceremonious style."

"I fail to see a connection,"
I said with some restraint.
He said, "It is in the protection
Of my blue and greyish paint.

"My closet is a little frayed
And in need of some repair
And the lovely coloured paint I made
Should provide some extra care.

"But first I need to test it
And eliminate the doubt
So here in joyful transit
I intent to try it out."

I uttered, "That's all very well, sir,
But why bother with the flea?"
He angered, "Why, cannot you tell, sir? –
Pray listen more carefully to me! –

"A dollop of that paint of mine
I've smothered on the mite.
Now should the coat stay good and fine
I'll know my plan was right –

"But should the paint chip and crack
As this flea goes hop and hit
I will take the little creature back
And, with the closet, dispose of it."

"All right," I said, "I've had enough.
It makes no sense to me."
The man ran off in a huff
Calling to his flea.

The fat fiery furry cat

The fat fiery furry cat
Fights like a fearless foe,
Looming like a lavish loon,
Leaving low-life low,
Wildly walking where she wants,
Awaking wanton woe.

The fat fiery furry cat
Finds fighting fine it seems,
Taking time to tease the tots
And test the timid teams,
Quelling kings of quiet qualms
And quenching quibbling queens.

The fat fiery furry cat
Says if you freedom-fight you'll fail,
And with tempers torn this tiger-like type
Teems of terror from top to tail,
Giving glaring ghastly growls
As she gusts of grit and gale.

All other fat and furry cats
Flag falsetto in her sight,
Marching madly many a mile
To miss her morbid might,
Through runs and rears and rends and rolls,
To rustle wrong from right.

But should you meet this feline fiend
Try smiling pleasantly
For though some say they'd rather leave
Than like a loser be,
And others, that fortune favours those
Who from such fierce flames flee –

I say she needs a little love,
That's all she needs, does she.

A person not always quite there

A person not always quite there
Lived down on his knees by a chair –
At least most of him did,
The rest of him hid
In the hall of his cousin named Claire.

A close encounter of the furred kind

Came a cry from the other room,
"Look at the size of that!"
And there he was on a chair
Staring at a rat –

Quivering and sweating
With a chattering of the teeth,
And he nearly climbed the wall
When it walked right underneath.

I thought my dad was fearless,
But no, I was not right.
And he stayed up there until that rat
Was clearly out of sight.

Oddies

Darren Dudley Dorking Brown
Lived beneath his eiderdown
Sitting there by day and night
Out of mind and out of sight.

Norman Norfolk Norbert Jones
Habitually digested stones.
When gross indulgence caused him pain
He'd spit them out at Aunty Jayne.

Brian Bedlam Barnsley Smythe
Thought it fun to steal a hive.
He took it homeward full of bees,
And sad to say released a sneeze.

Hannah Hanley Hilda Slater –
And in her bath, an alligator.
A lot of room in there it lacks,
But it's very good for scrubbing backs.

Bessie Biteyerlegsoff Gray
Left her home and ran away.
Few though will applaud the fact
Least one day she journey back.

Martin Matlock Maudlin Lyle
Sent his friend a crocodile,
But it's funny how he can't explain
Why he's never seen his friend again.

Wayne Wyoming Whitlock Pugh
Soaked his hands in rabbit glue,
Stuck himself to his own front door
And shouted, "I've been here before!"

Oddies here, oddies there,
Oddies living everywhere.
Everyone has oddie ways –
At some of mine you'd be amazed.

for older ones

I appear to have disappeared

I appear to have disappeared,
There is nothing left of me,
And all because I caused a scene
When we were having tea.

Now everyone looks through me,
But there are benefits, no doubt –
For I can do what I like
Without them finding out.

Most contributions welcome

The vicar was not very happy,
But the box read, "For the sick." –
And Dad had downed six pints that day
And he needed something quick

The Dulcet Bird

The Dulcet Bird – an unusual thing –
It gestures there with upturned wing
And utterly refuses to sing
Despite its reputation.

It's plump and green both front and back,
It doesn't trill, it doesn't quack –
It simply has this special knack
Of rousing folks' frustration.

High above upon a tree,
Its beak shut quite indignantly,
Aloof for all the world to see,
This scourge of the nation –

The sweetest bird
You've never heard,
Sitting there, most absurd,
Like a lump of vegetation.

Mum sez I hav da gift

Isnt Rory ugly?
Is spts r so rvltng.
Mel sed Im a stpd cow.
Shes so inslting.

Jadz splt up wit Simon.
2nite wont need a lft,
Ive gt piano lesnz.
Mum sez I hav da gift.

Id b us wit me fngrs –
Wot wll she tink of nxt?
Beta go Ive spnt $^1/_2$ a min
Typng u dis txt.

I should not share my underpants

I should not share my underpants
With anyone but me –
And if you saw the skid marks there
I think you would agree.

No amount of washing
Ever makes them clean.
They are the only things I own
That I would call obscene.

Two old gents

Two old gents sitting there
Rocking to and fro –
Very sad that in this world
They should be quite so.

One was once a soldier,
A hero in the war,
In the days when life, it seemed,
Was worth the fighting for.

The other was a sailor,
Sailed the oceans blue –
Now they sit, wasting time,
Rocking fro and to.

You won't like it, but the dust mite...

What a revolting thing is the dust mite;
We cater for all of his needs;
On the fallen dead skin from our bodies
This being continuously feeds.

He's so small we never can see him
And he's ugly, and although tiny, he's fat –
And he lives on the shelves, in the bedclothes,
On the carpet, the rug and the mat.

And a million or more of these creatures
Is the total in every bed,
Excited as we go to join them,
Knowing they're soon to be fed.

Generations of parents and children
And cousins and nephews and nieces –
And it's not surprising we suffer from asthma
When we keep inhaling their faeces.

My great uncle is just short of eighty
With no wife and no intimate friend,
But at least the common old dust mite
Will sleep with him right to the end.

Our zombie nation

What did we do back in those days
Before the mobile found us?
Ah yes, I can remember now –
We talked to those around us.

Little Dippy Dora

She's three sheets to the wind –
You'd know it if you saw 'er –
Things aren't quite right up there
With Little Dippy Dora.

She's lost the plot,
All my friends ignore 'er –
She's harmless, but she's hopeless
Is Little Dippy Dora.

But she is a kindly soul,
I will say that for 'er –
So please show her some respect,
My Little Dippy Dora.

The art of missspelling

I'm getting beta at it,
It's a nack I lernt at skool.
My teechers weer not bovered
And swottin wasant kool.

Beesides it doesant matta
In this computor age –
I can press the spellcheque buttan
Arfta finnishing the paige.

Thoughts whilst studying

Sitting with my homework,
Breathing acid rain,
Reading up on some old war
We once fought out with Spain.

I wonder – all this fighting –
What is it all about?
Disputing every border
And they never sort it out.

Life is full of problems –
What do we live it for?
We all get hurt, we run away
And then we all come back for more.

But it's hard for me to concentrate
In the sultry winter air –
The temperatures go up and up,
And no one seems to care.

And there's pollution all around us –
It's everywhere, but why?
So I stare out from my window
And contemplate the sky.

Perhaps there's life beyond the Earth,
Perhaps another Spain
To befriend another England
And live to fight again.

On Venus, if life is there,
It can't be carbon based –
But who's to say that other forms
Of life might yet be traced?

On Titan, on the freezing ground,
Beneath the swirling mists,
There's still a chance, be it remote,
That some basic life exists.

And there may be life inside the Moon
And there may be life on Mars
And there must be all sorts of life
On worlds between the stars.

These thoughts I sit and ponder
As I wonder what life's worth –
And I wonder too, in fifty years,
Will there still be life on Earth?

I'm going on a diet

I'm going on a diet –
I've had enough of this –
It's now so far from me to you
That we can't even kiss.

If proof were needed

I upset my parents yesterday –
They made me sit in silence –
I hired out another film
With lots of scenes of violence.

They said that many experts claim
It can affect the way we act –
Well if I had my way those experts
Would be beaten up and sacked.

Coming to terms

The first day back at school –
I hate it with a passion.
That awful uniform again –
You would hardly call it fashion.

Getting up so early,
Eating breakfast super quick,
Rushing in for nothing –
It's enough to make you sick.

I don't need education,
I can manage life without.
My dad can earn a living
By knowing next to nowt.

A good run

"Art thou weary, art thou languid,
Art thou sore distressed?" –
Did Mum wash your five white shirts
In with your bright red vest?

But there is no need to vex yourself –
It's not as bad as you might think –
At least when you're at school each day
You'll be in the pink.

There was a young fellow from Spain

There was a young fellow from Spain
Who was surprisingly partial to pain.
When he fell off a cliff,
Although battered and stiff,
He got up and shouted "Again!"

Into gaming?

Into gaming? Hooked on gaming?
Can't put that console down?
Only stopping for the toilet
Or another game from town?

When you turn off the light
Is the screen there in your head?
Then before it is too late for you
Try reading books instead.

There was a young fellow from Surrey

There was a young fellow from Surrey
Who consumed several kilos of curry.
He went to work the next day,
But was only half way
When he had to go back in a hurry.

I hate the letter 'n'

I hate the letter "n" –
When you think it starts a word
You find that there's a "k" or "g" –
It really is absurd.

It messes up my "knickers",
My "gnome", my "knee", my "gnat",
My "knack", my "knight", my "knock" –
And "know", it ruins that –

And "gnat" and "gnaw" and "knead" and "knife"
And "knit" and "knell" and "knot" –
Whoever invented spelling,
They wrote a load of rot.

On verbal diarrhoea

"At this particular moment in time,"
Said my teacher, but do tell me how
She was allowed to use so many words
When all she was saying was "Now."

If we could shorten the sentences teachers use
School days could be cut down by hours;
Then we could spend more time in our beds,
Chilling out or soaping in showers.

A man from somewhere out west

A man from somewhere out west
Always wore the same pants and vest,
But after years in the garments
Even inhabiting varmints
Were frankly quite far from impressed.

Thoughts in a bath

They're poking through the bubbles,
At my command they move -
I suppose they are a part of me,
But I strongly disapprove.

All my other areas
Are delicate and neat –
If bodies have to have an end
Why must it be in feet?

Giggling Gertie

I upset the new bus driver,
She really got quite shirty,
But to diffuse the situation
Along came Giggling Gertie.

I fell over in a puddle,
I got all wet and dirty,
But then to make things better
Along came Giggling Gertie.

"Don't get back late," Mum said.
I got home at eleven-thirty –
It's a good job I had the sense
To bring back Giggling Gertie.

At first I was a zygote

At first I was a zygote,
But not some creature from the stars –
No, this was just the product
Formed from cells of Ma's and Pa's.

Then I became a blastocyst,
A ring of cells in my Mum's womb,
Like a little tiny titchy thing
Inside a darkened tomb.

Next off I was an embryo,
My brain was taking form –
There I was all comfortable
Floating snug and warm.

Then I was a foetus
Growing day by day,
New bits of me all popping out
In each and every way.

Then I became a baby,
An arrival in the World,
Screaming in the open –
Alive, alert, uncurled.

And now I am a growing lad
With the rest of life ahead,
With all the mysteries of life
To solve inside my head.

And then the wind changed

"Don't make a face like that!"
My grandad said to me.
"If the wind decides to change
You'll stay like that – you'll see!"

"Don't be silly!" I replied.
"You're just senile and deranged!"
And I pulled another face at him –
And then the wind changed.

What is it with teachers?

What is it with teachers? –
They roar and rant and rave.
It's almost as if they're out to get
Themselves an early grave.

All that constant worry
Must make them feel quite queasy.
It's not their education
So they ought to take it easy.

How long is a yonk?

How long is a yonk?
For ages I've vexed.
If you know the answer
Please give me a text.

A donkey should know,
It lives all those years,
But it holds on to its secrets –
Or so it appears.

So will I ever find out?
Sad to say I'm in doubt.
Could this yonk be as long
As it takes to find out?

Camels are mammals

Camels are mammals,
Humans are too –
But humans are mammals
That visit the zoo.

In conversation with a dot

"I'm the best!"

"Oh, no you're not!"

"What I say is never absurd
And the world hangs on to my every word."

"Whatever you say, be it apt or neat,
Without me it is incomplete."

"You're just a splodge upon the page –
I'm a glorious product of the age –
In intellectual terms I am at the top." –

"I've had enough of this – full stop!"

My diet - you should try it

In my opinion crockery
Should never harbour broccoli.
Indeed all things green
Are blatantly obscene.

Bread and chips and meat –
They make my life complete.
A burger in a bun –
That's my idea of fun.

And I remove all lettuce lurking
And discard that dreadful gherkin.
All right, I might be unhealthy and fat,
But I can learn to live with that.

O to be less weedy

O to be less weedy
And not some skinny rake!
What chance have I of pulling
Like this, for Heaven's sake?

There's this girl in Year Eleven,
She turns my glasses steamy,
But I bet if I went up to her
She wouldn't even see me.

I like my fellow earthlings

I like my fellow Earthlings,
They make my life complete –
Some of them I cuddle
And some of them I eat.

Saturday was father's day

Saturday was father's day,
He took me to the park,
And there we kicked a ball around
Till it was nearly dark.

He's quite good at it really,
But I always seem to win,
And I knew, when he started panting,
That it was time to pack it in.

Then I said I'd like an ice cream
And as we stood there queuing
He asked, "How are you getting on
And how's your mother doing?"

I told him we were both okay
And he didn't have to worry.
He said he was going out that night
For a beer and curry.

And then he took me home again,
But left me at the door.
Funny things these adults –
Grown up yet immature.

Holy Cow!

A miraculous transformation,
Enough to make one shudder –
The grass goes in at one end,
The milk comes out the udder!

So fair and foul

You could tell what she was doing
When she gave a little cough –
It was an attempt to disguise it
When she had let one off.

And she was such a looker,
You would have stared so hard and long,
You would have worshipped such a beauty
Had it not been for the pong.

And boy they were fruity –
Lethal – and suffice to say
If I had made such stinkers
I'd have locked myself away.

Whenever there's a spider

Whenever there's a spider
We find my sister and we hide her.
We don't want the frustration
Of hyperventilation –
With all that running and ranting
And screaming and shouting and panting.
Not a bag round her mouth, but instead
We should put it right over her head.

Index of first lines